Coloring & Activity Books for Kids
"Fruits & Vegetable"

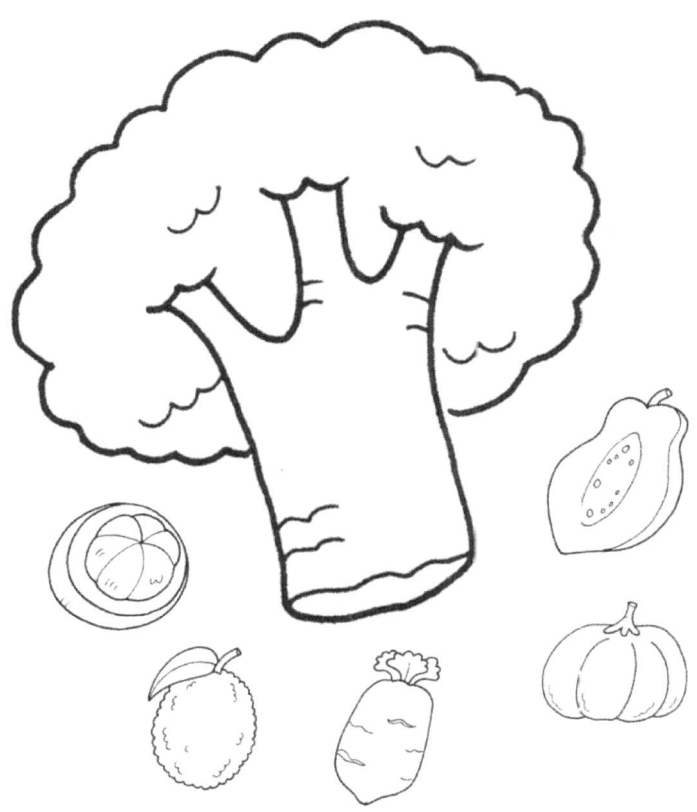

Jye Wynn

Coloring & Activity Books for Kids: Fruits & Vegetable

Copyright: Published in the United States by Author Name
Published March 2018

All rights reserved. No part of this publication may be reproduced, stored in retrieval system, copied in any form or by any means, electronic, mechanical, photocopying, recording or otherwise transmitted without written permission from the publisher. Please do not participate in or encourage piracy of this material in any way. You must not circulate this book in any format. Jye Wynn does not control or direct users' actions and is not responsible for the information or content shared, harm and/or actions of the book readers.

ISBN-13: 978-1986380188

ISBN-10: 1986380181

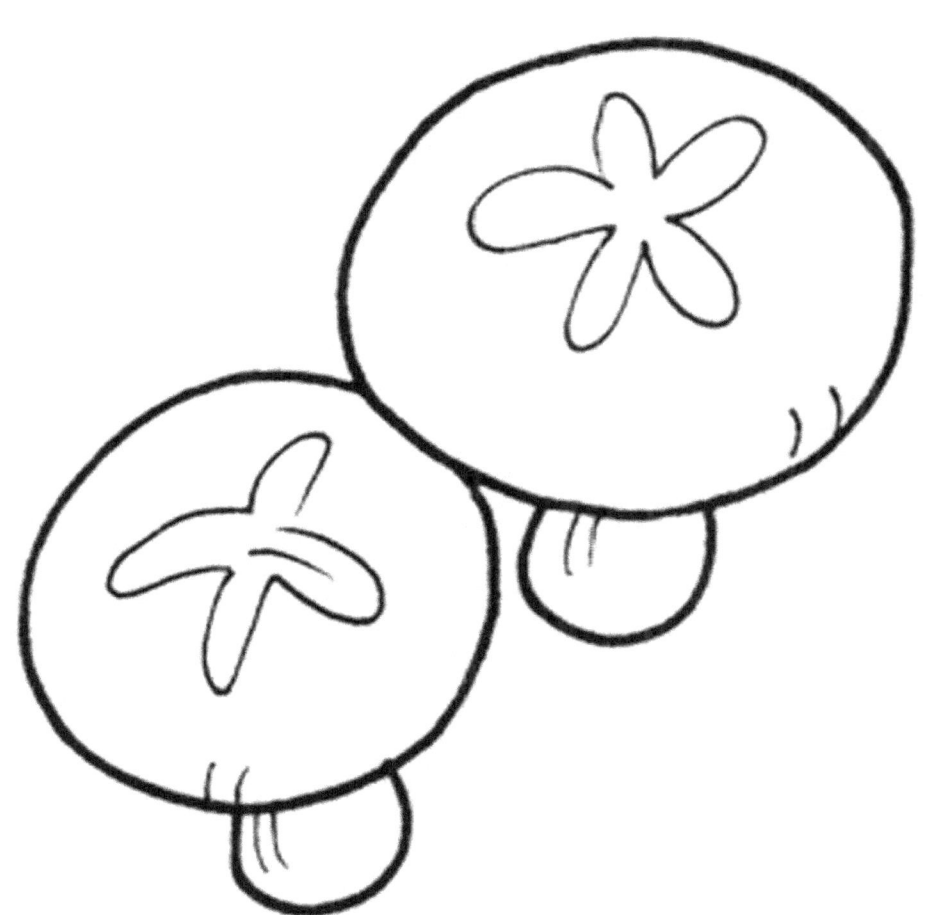

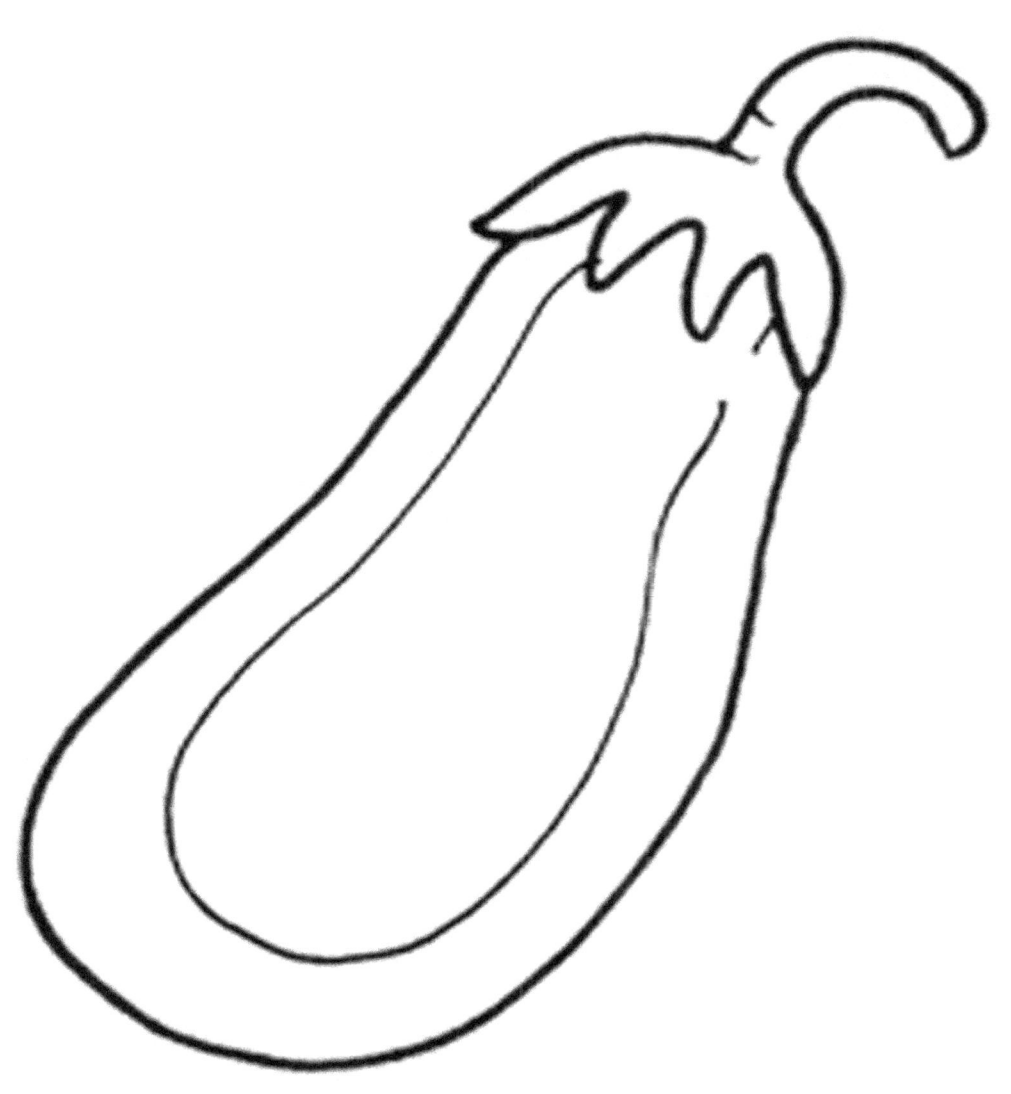

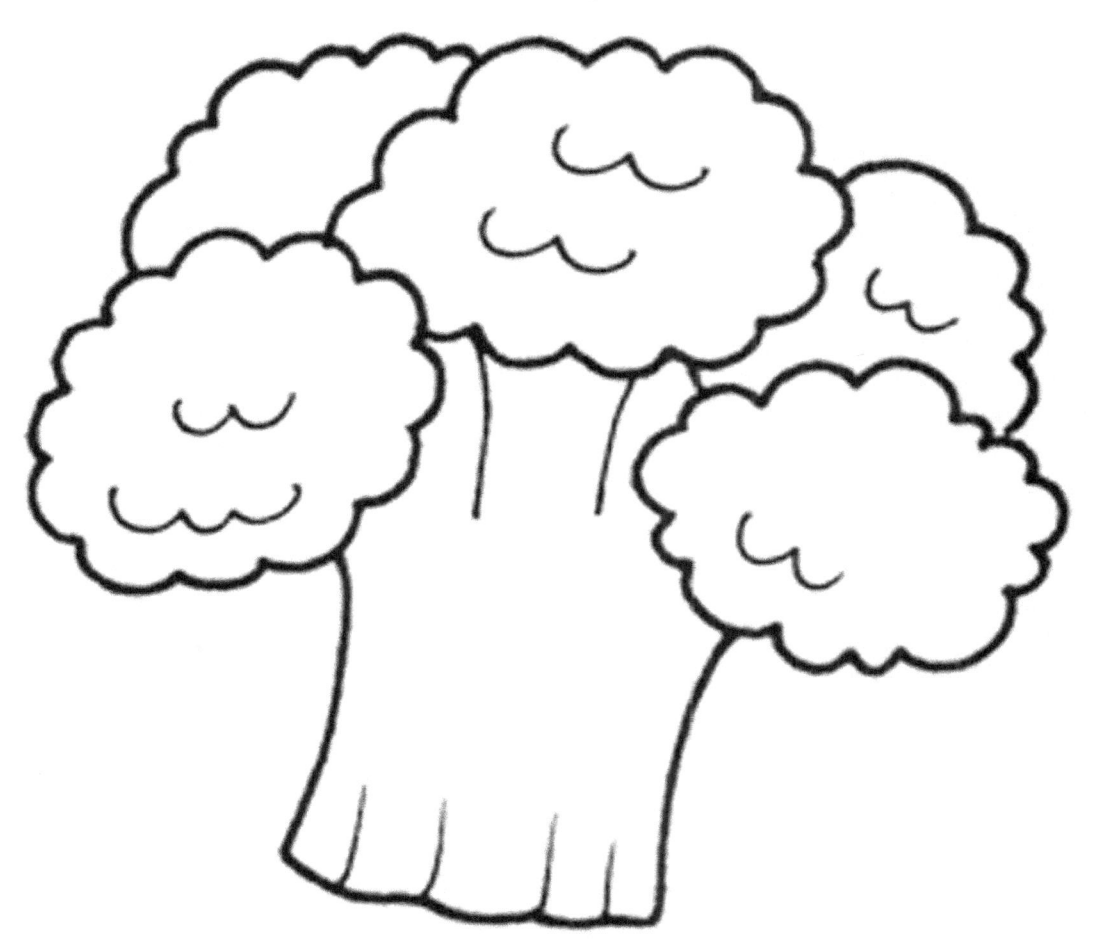

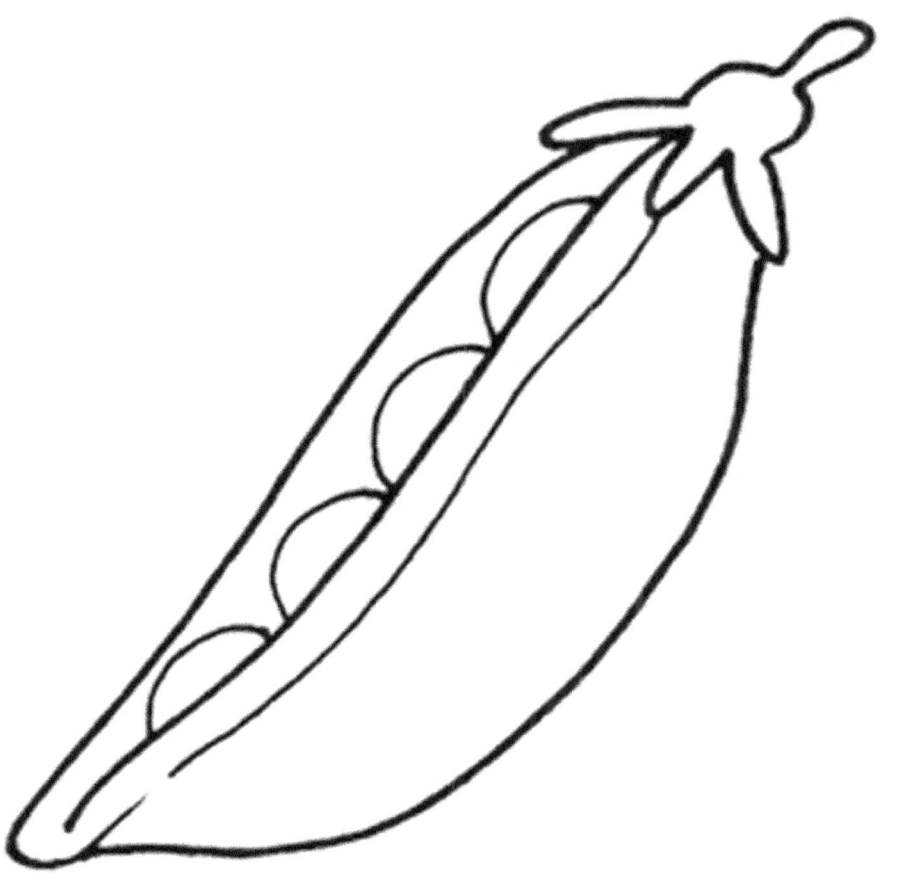

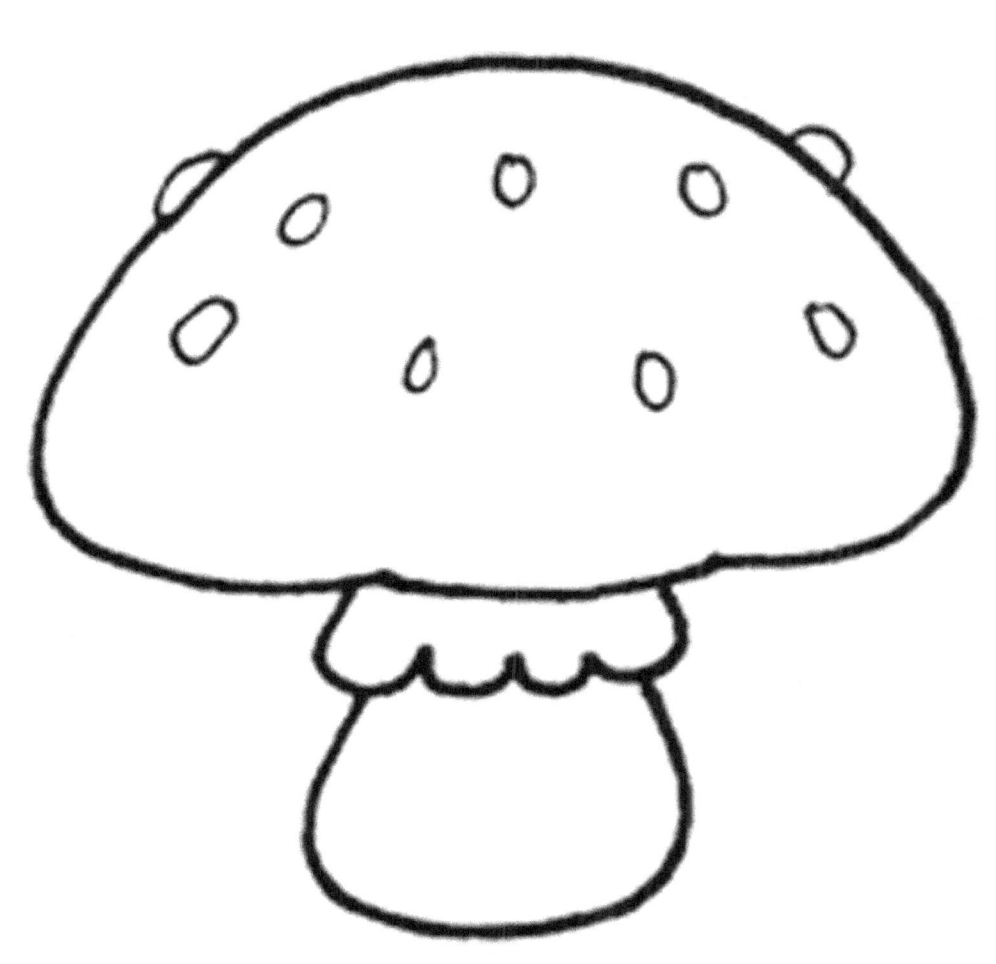

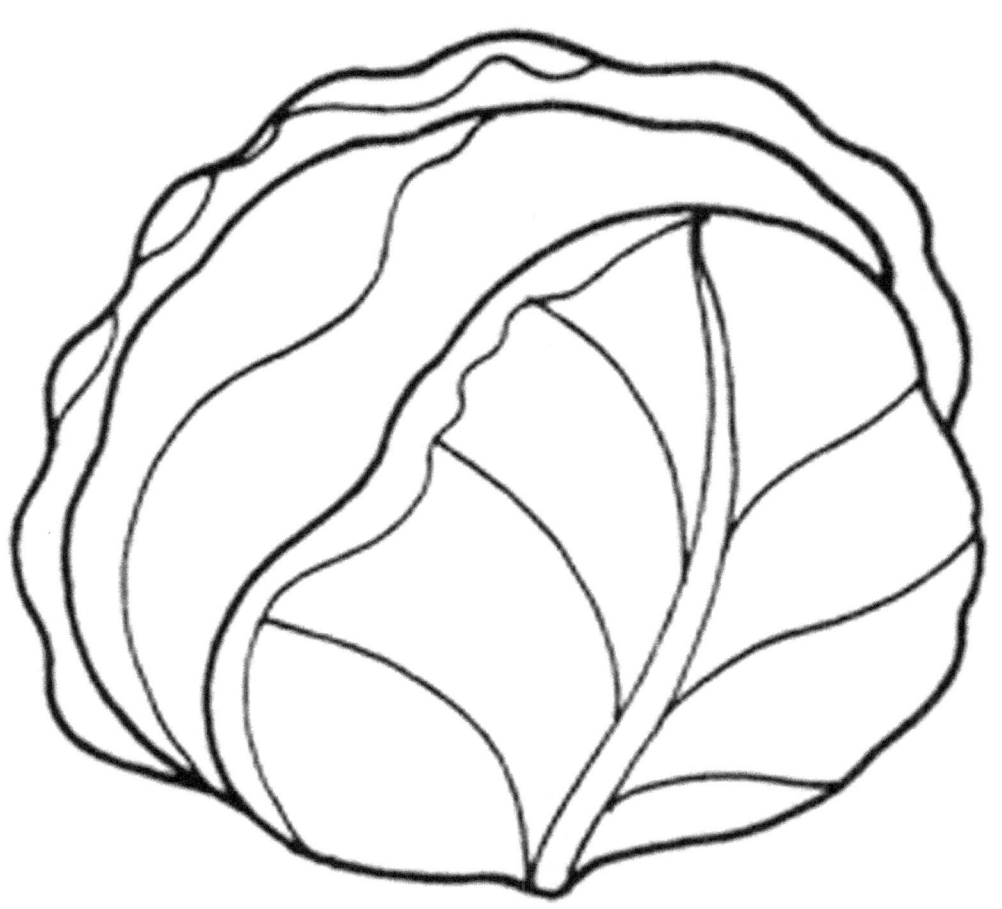

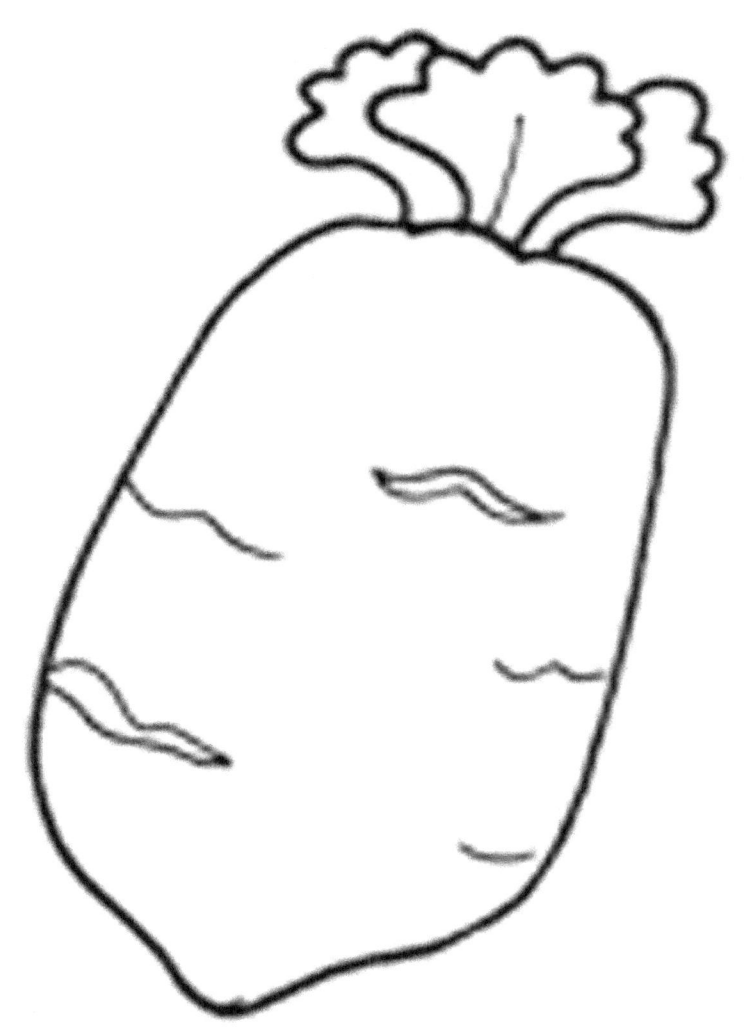

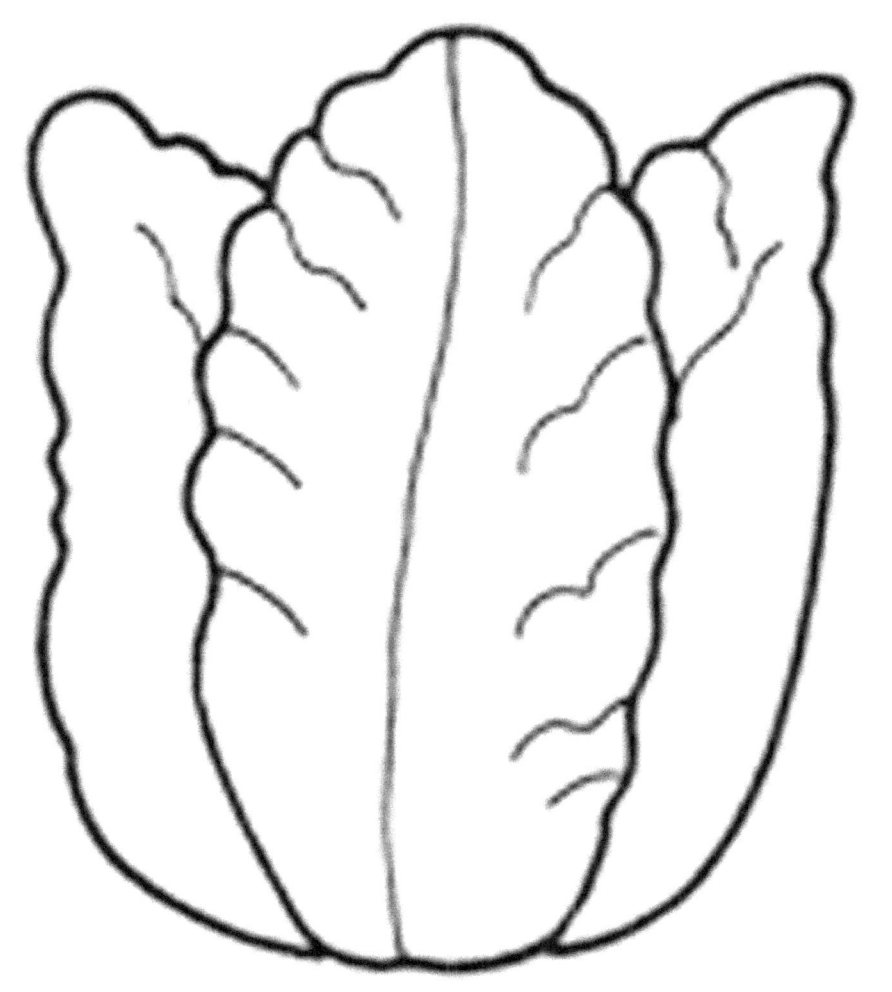

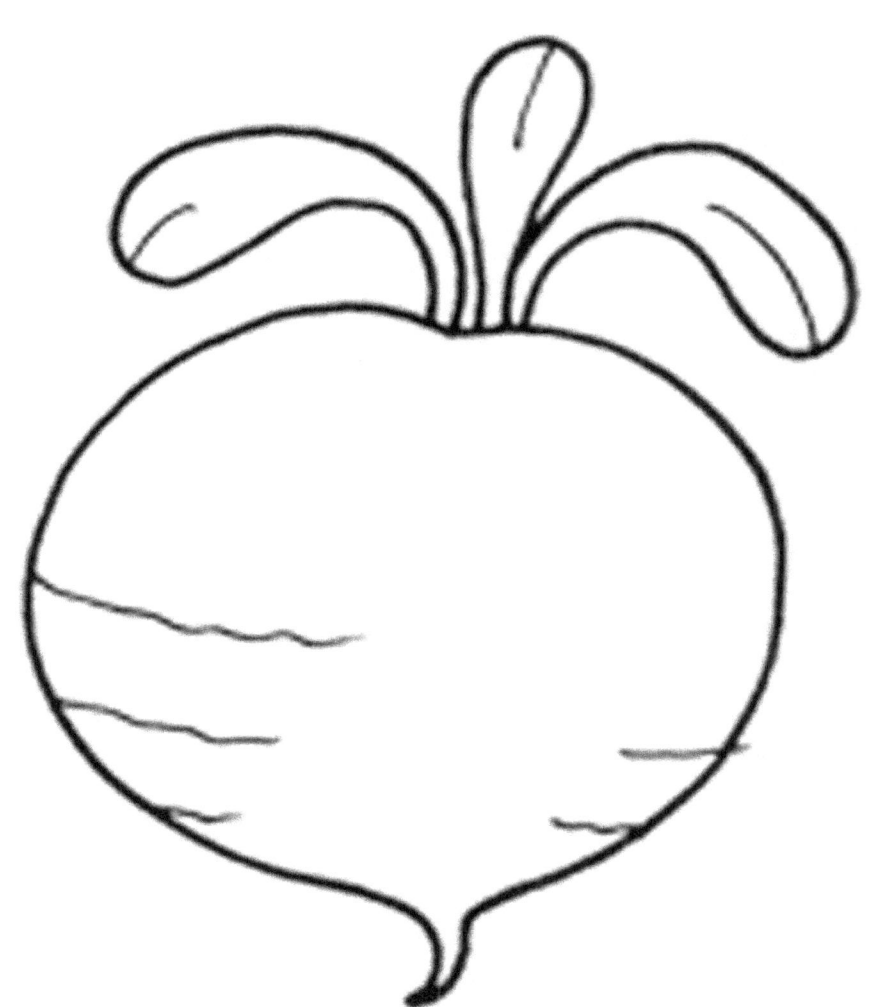

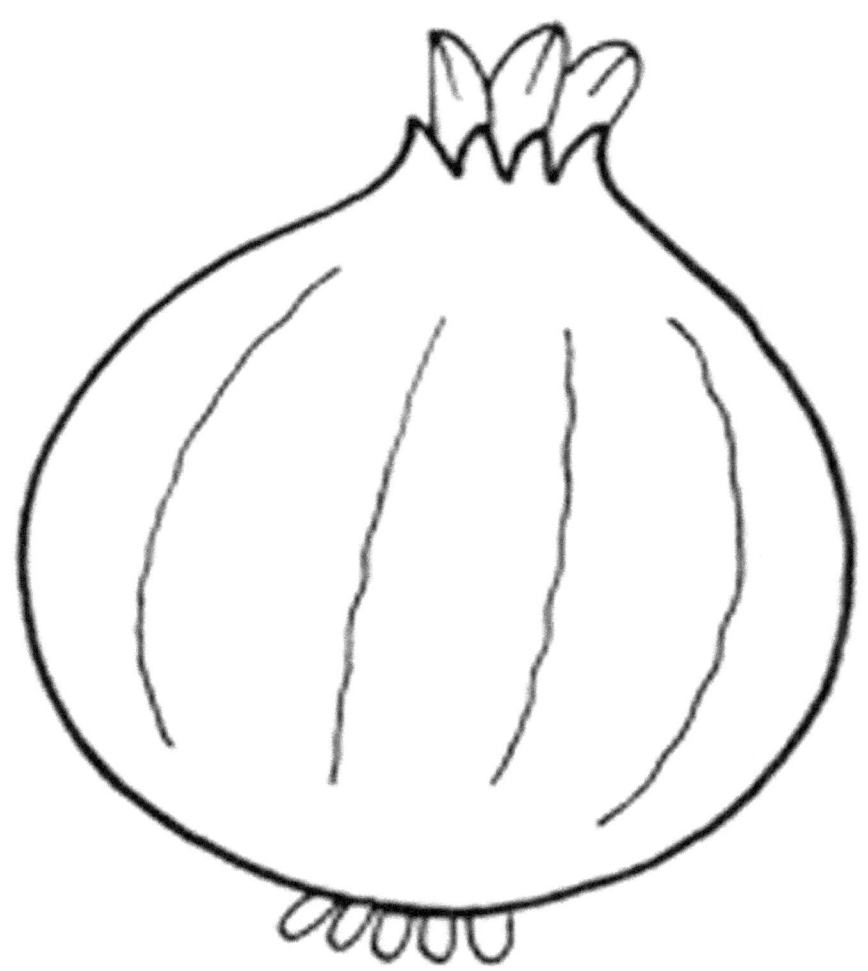

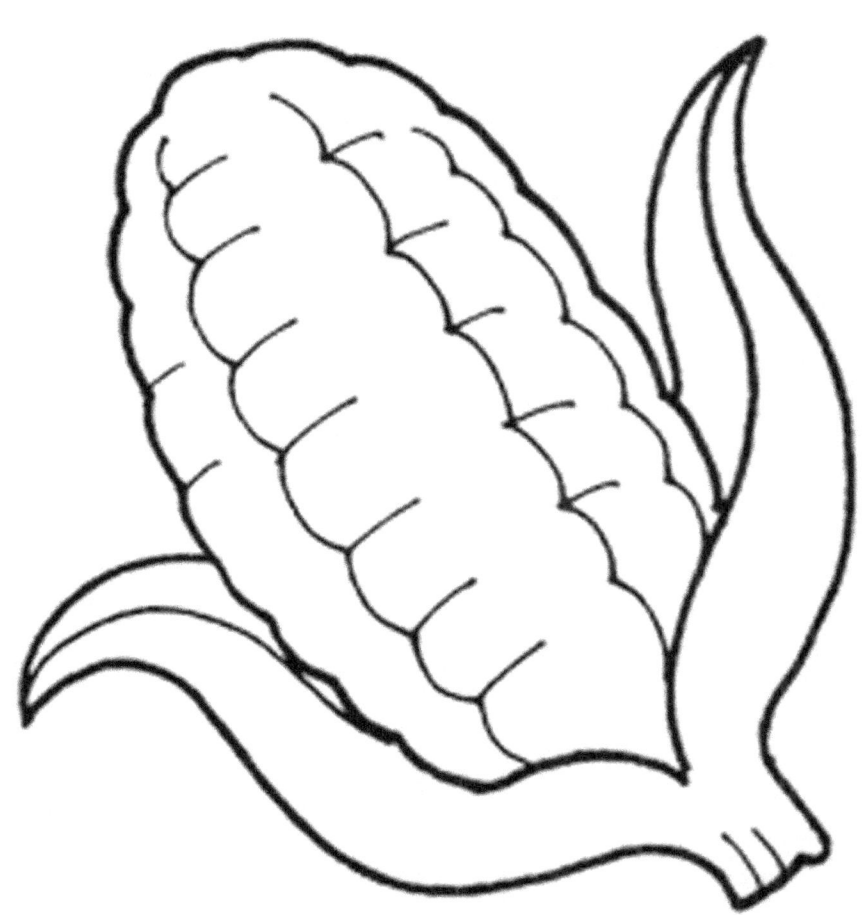

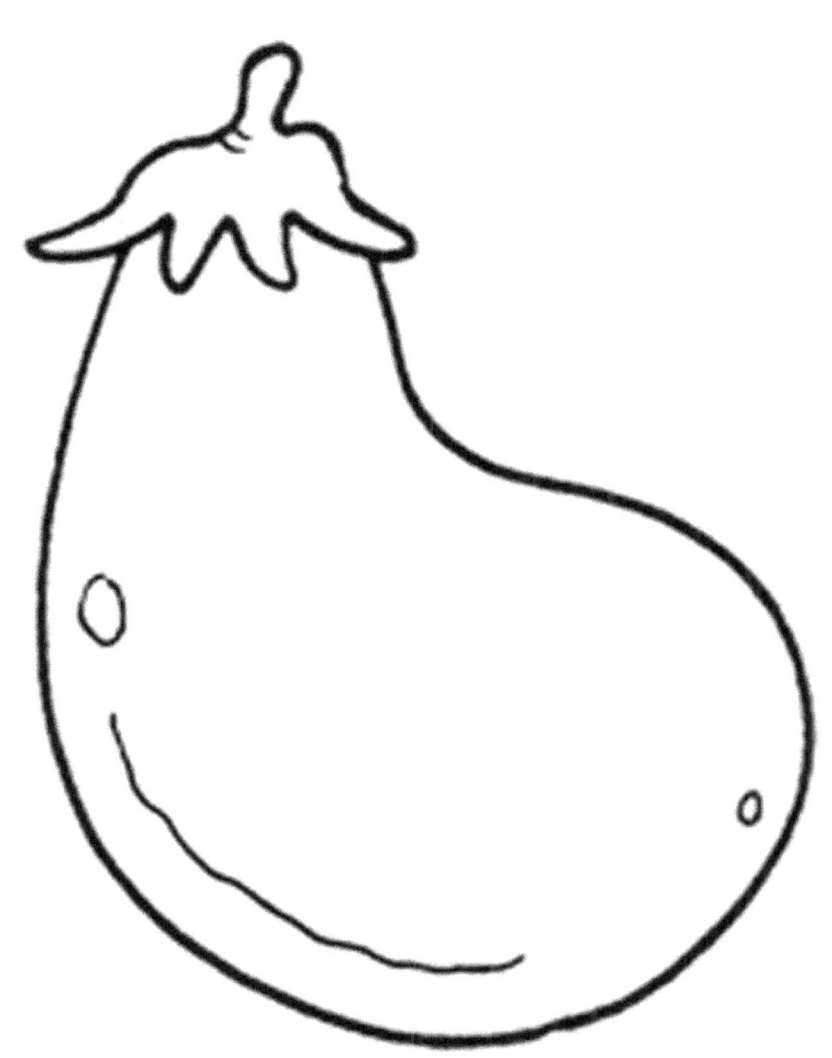

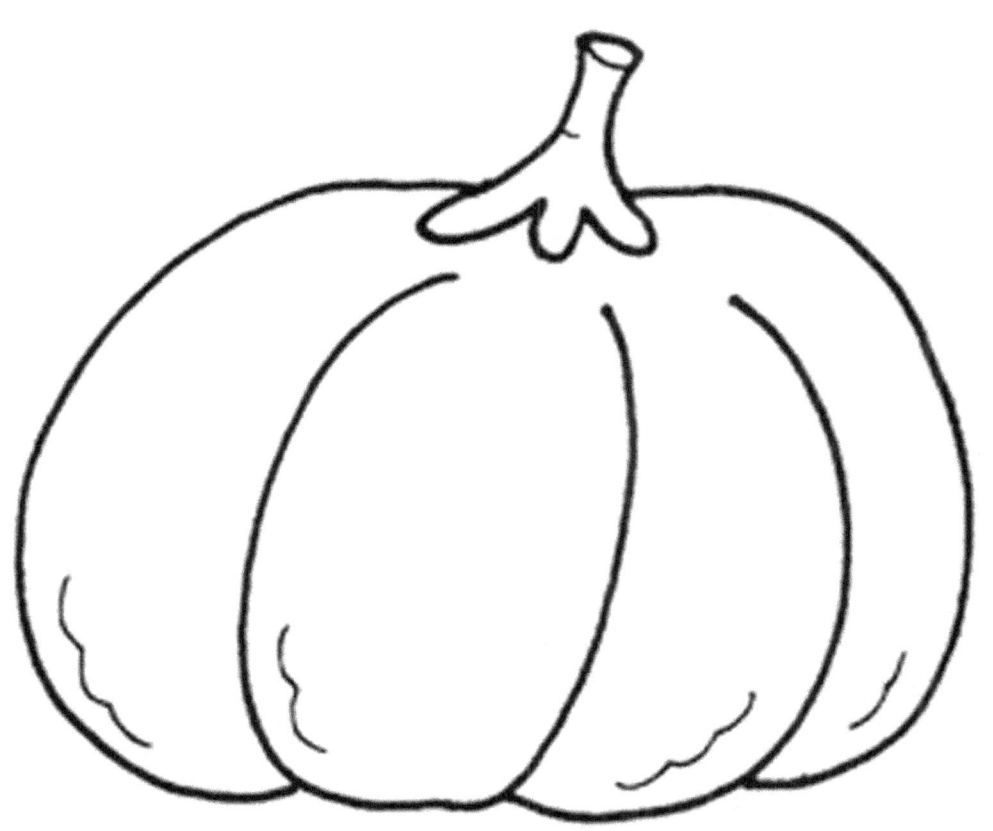

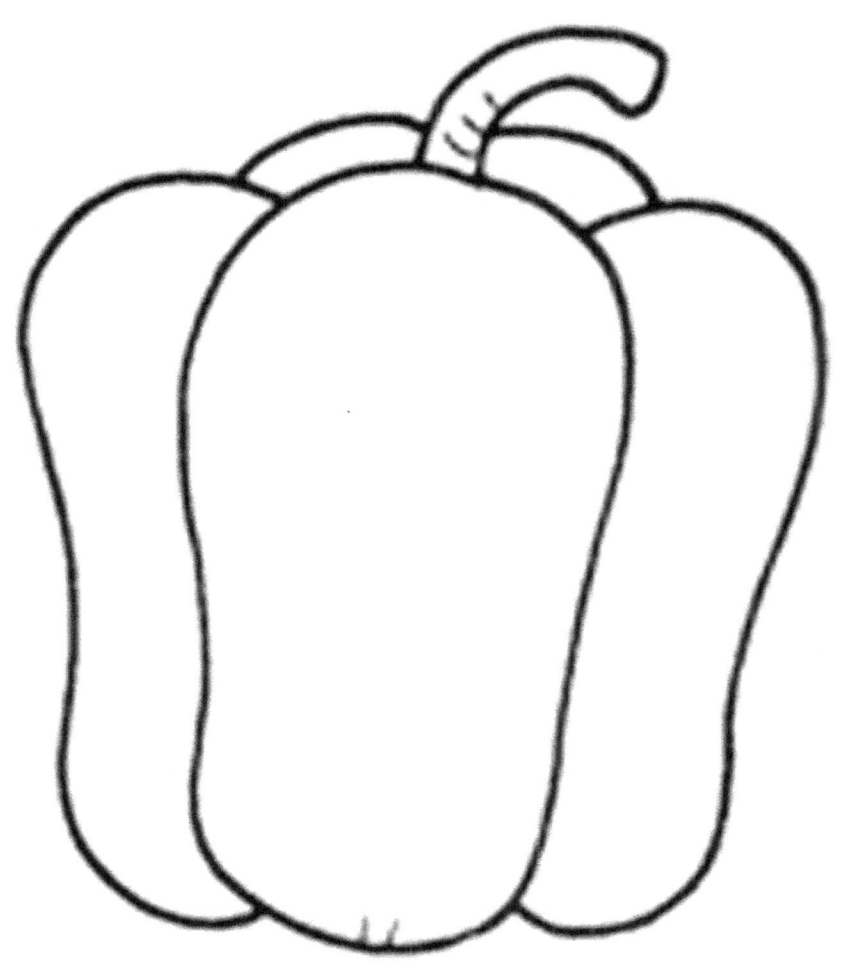

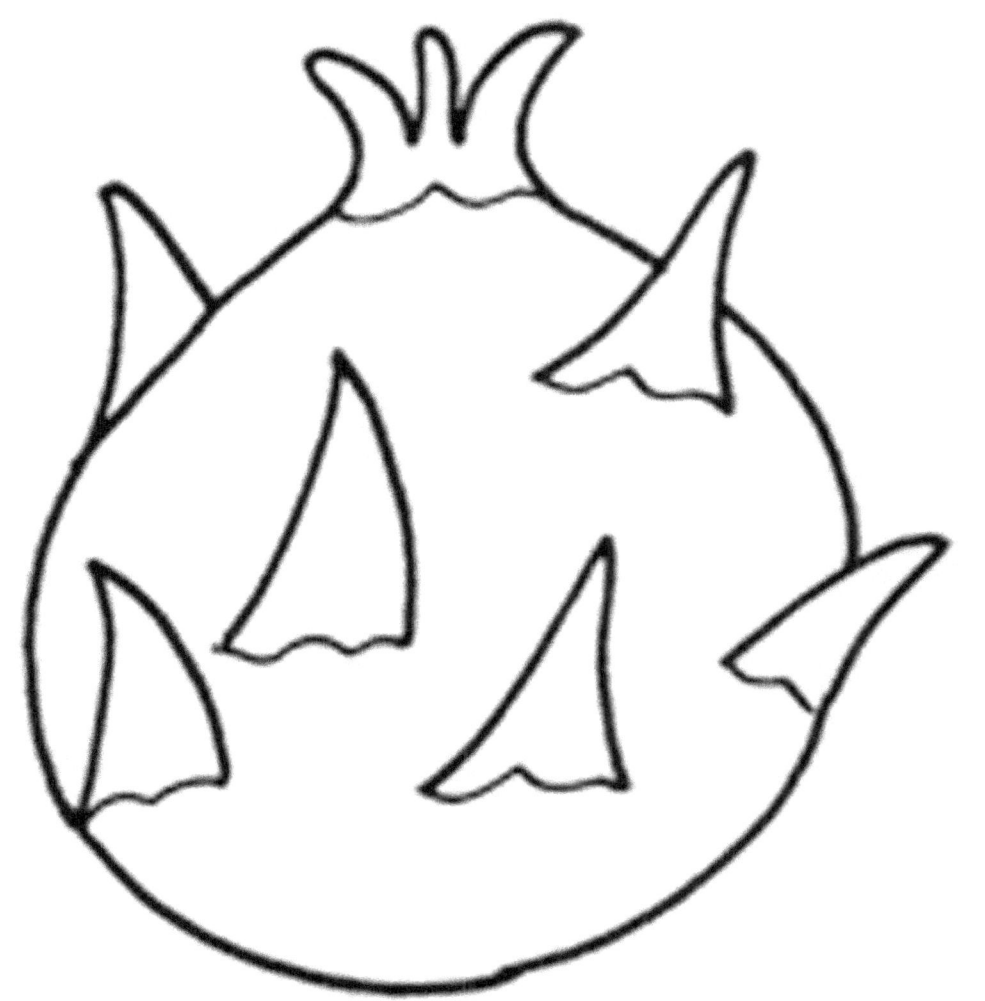

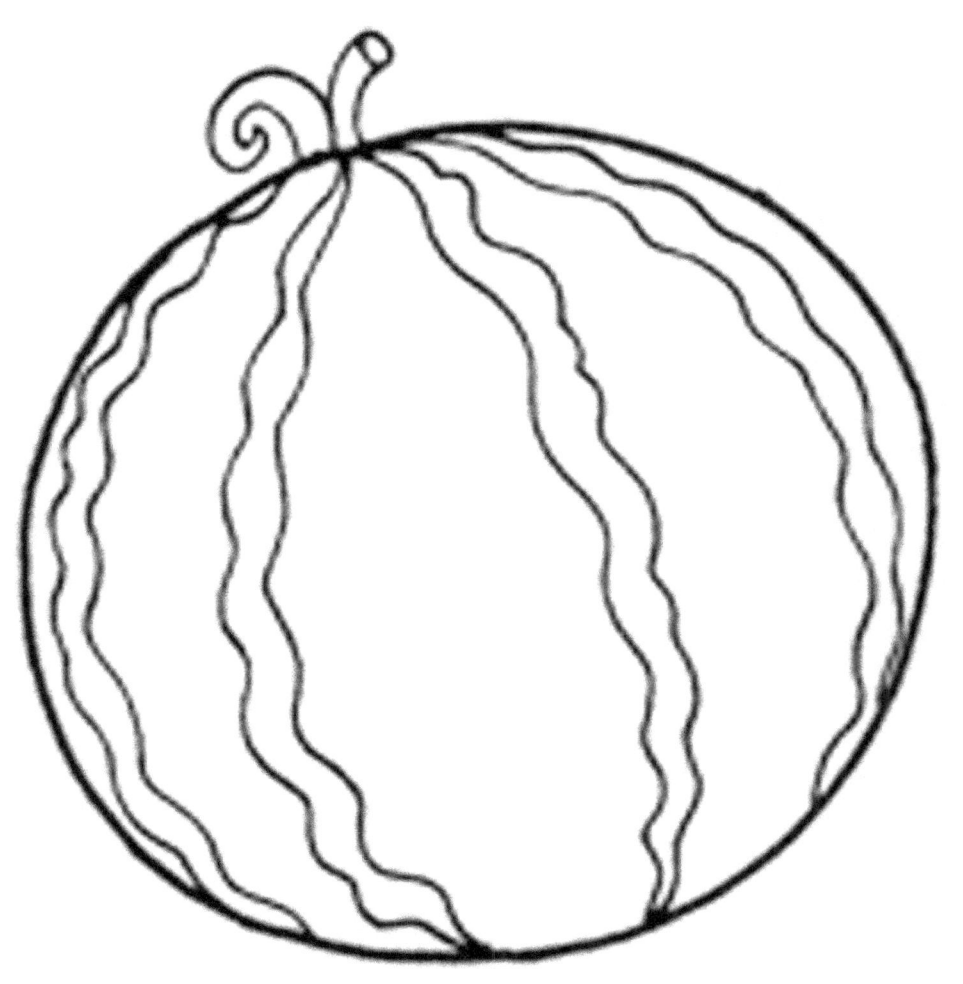

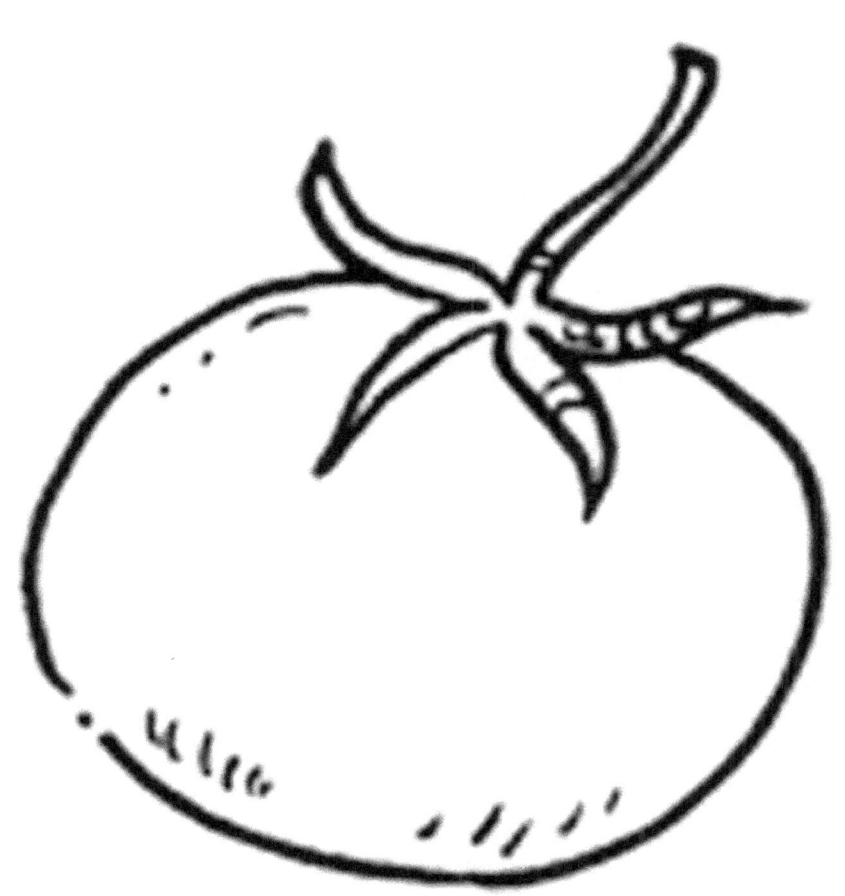

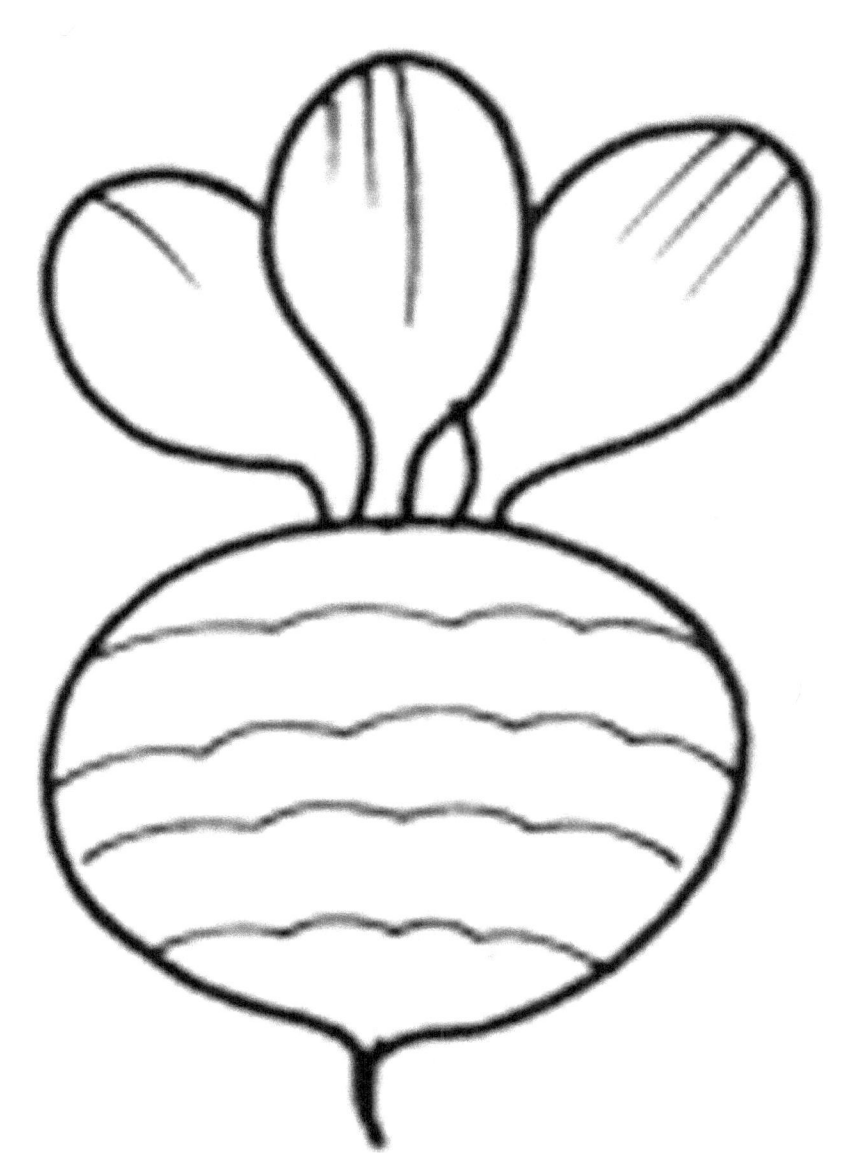

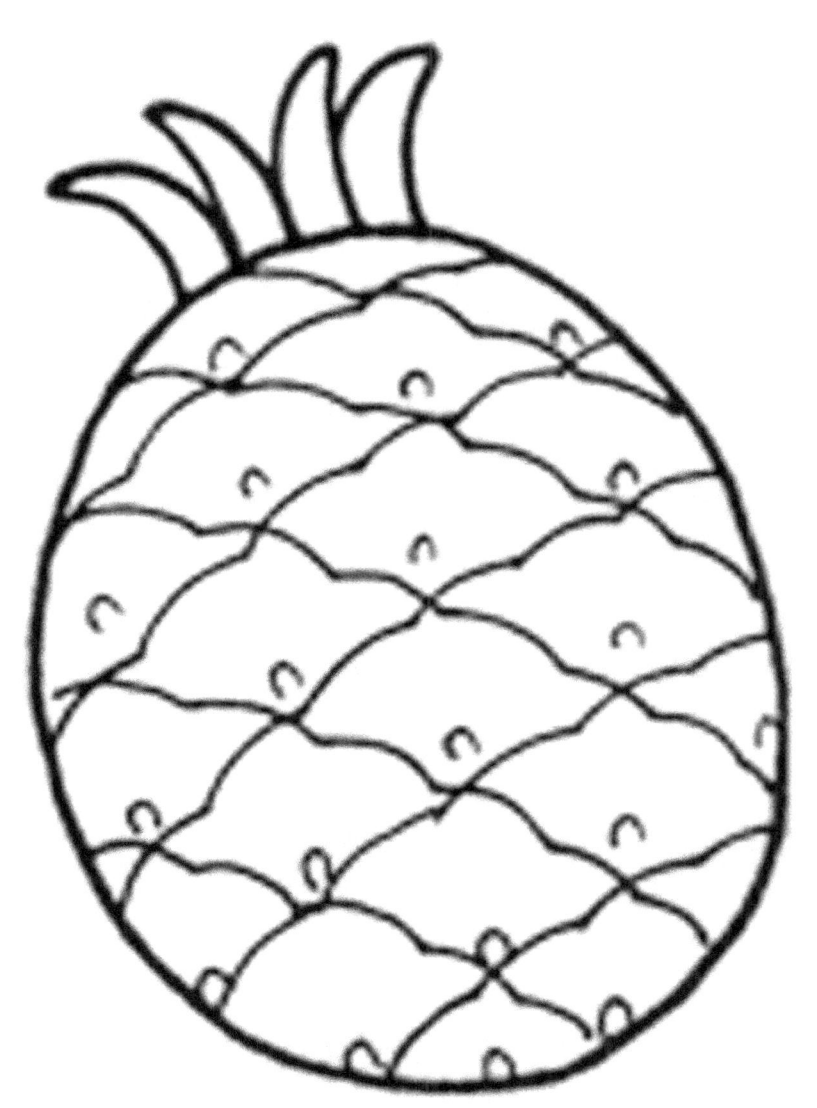

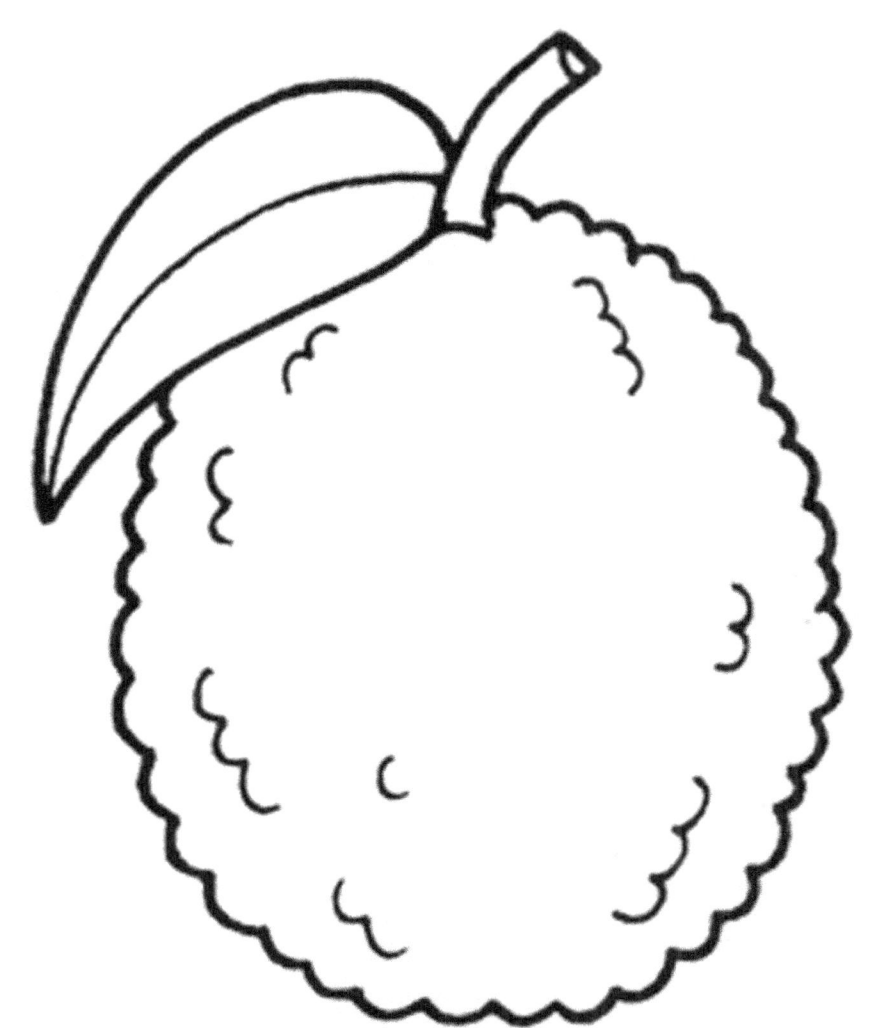

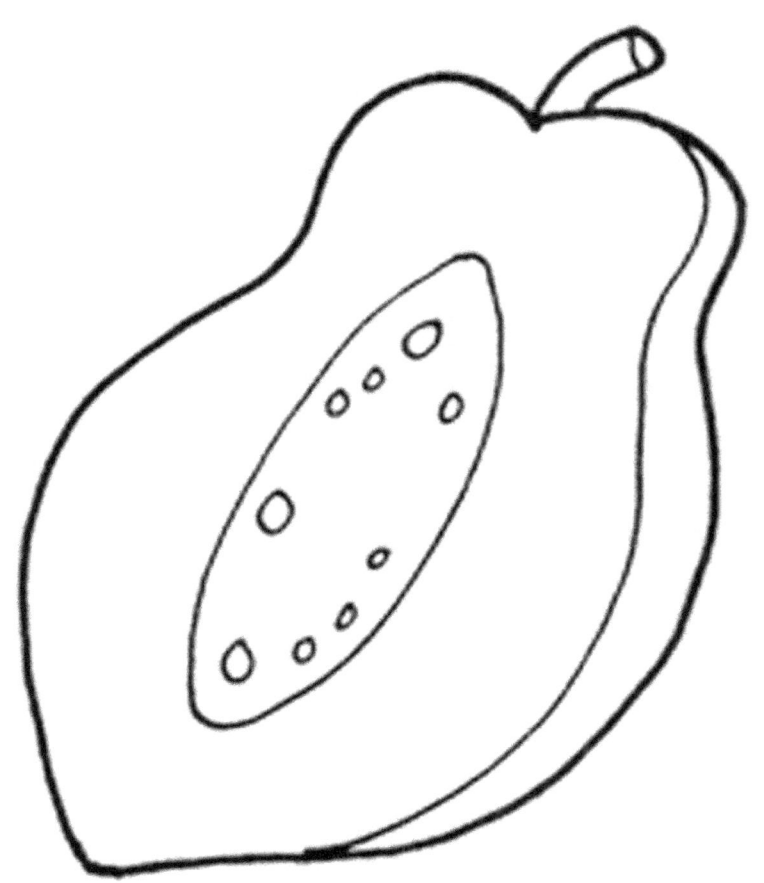

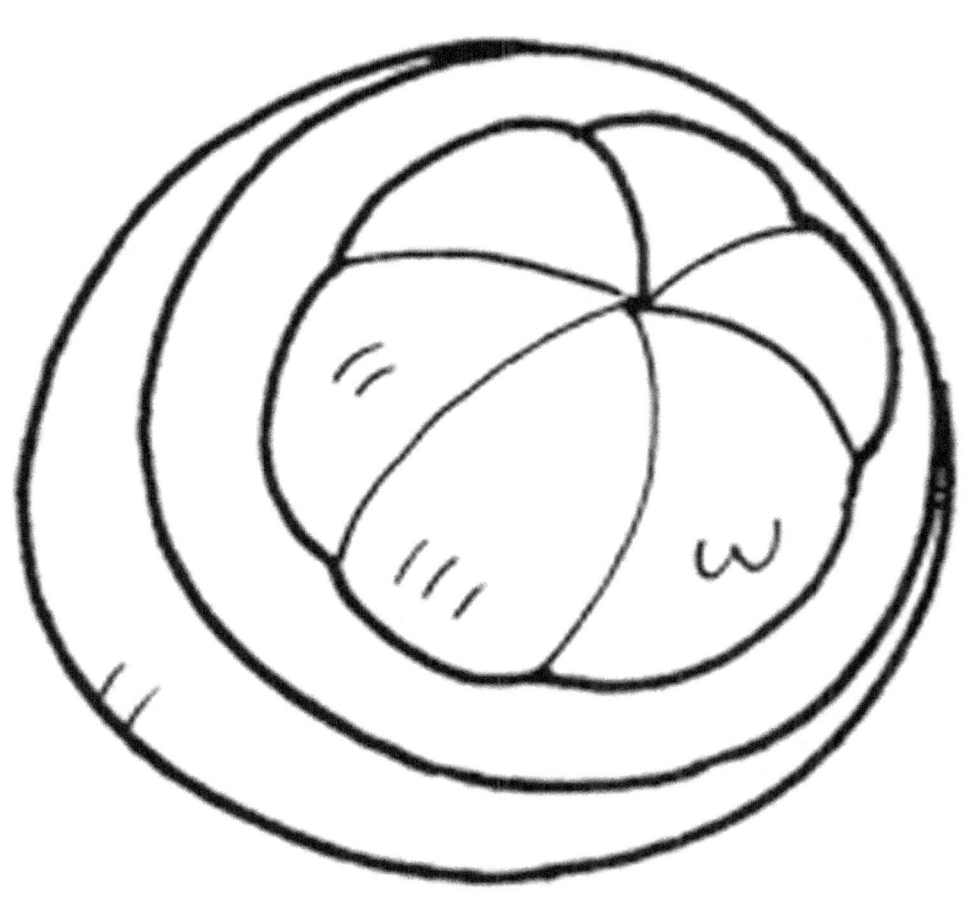

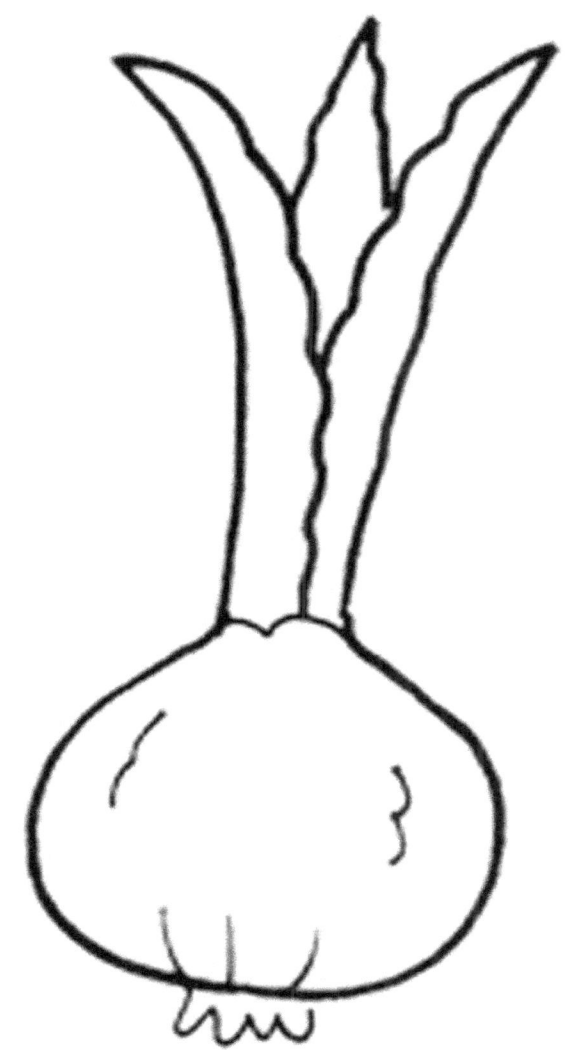

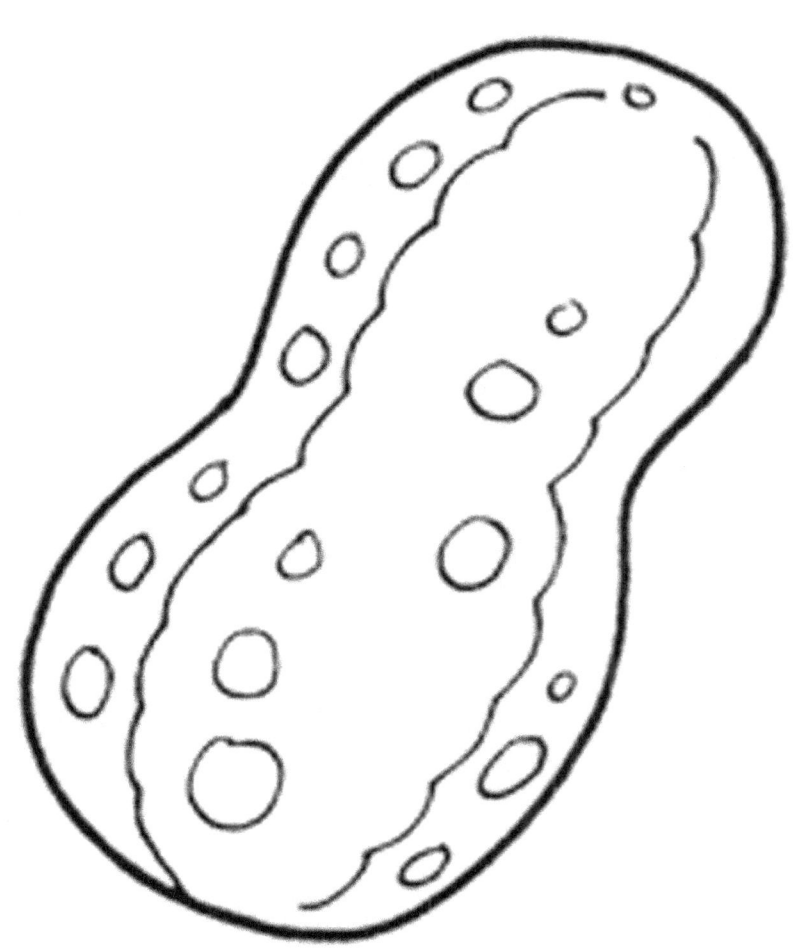

Thank you

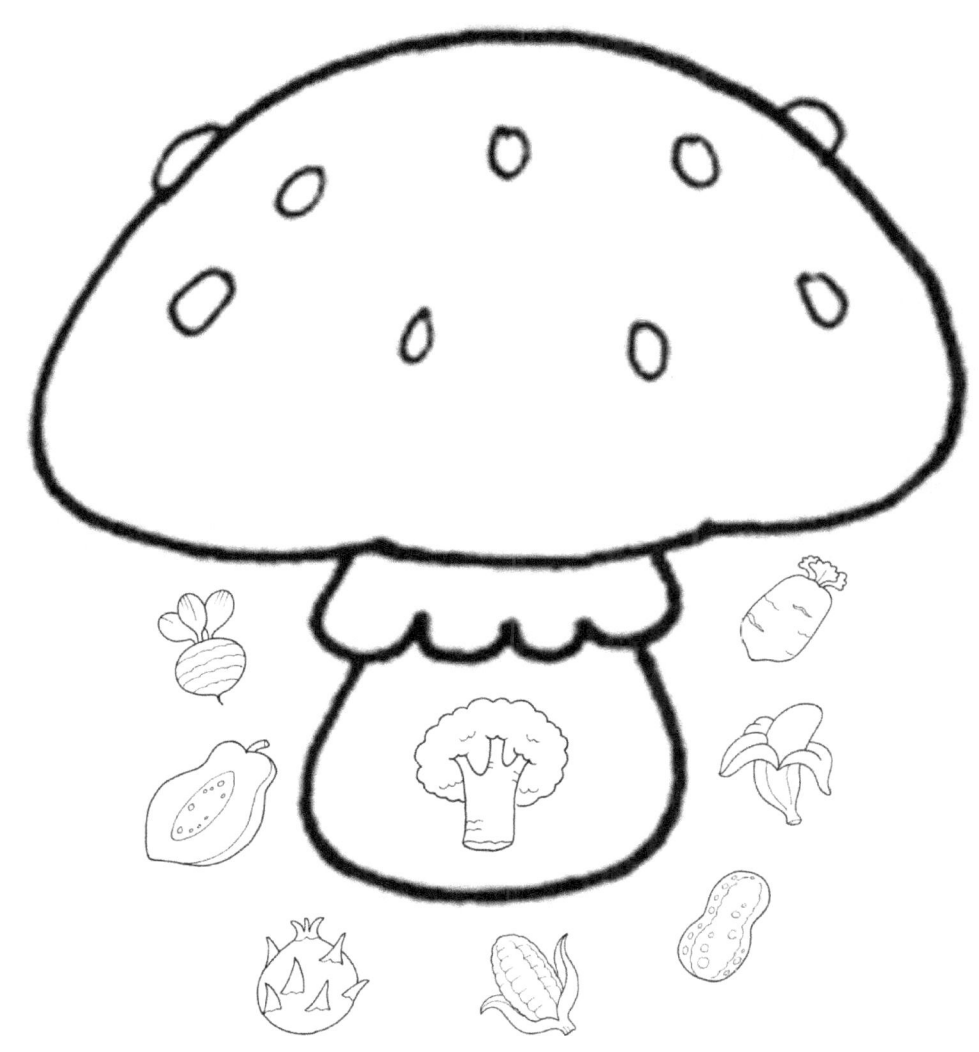

www.ingramcontent.com/pod-product-compliance
Lightning Source LLC
Chambersburg PA
CBHW062124220526
45471CB00010B/3867